THRILL SEEKERS

CLIMBING MOUNT EVEREST

WITHDRAWN

BY KRISTEN RAJCZAK

Gareth Stevens
Publishing

Please visit our website, www.garethstevens.com. For a free color catalog of all our high-quality books, call toll free 1-800-542-2595 or fax 1-877-542-2596.

Library of Congress Cataloging-in-Publication Data

Rajczak, Kristen.
Climbing Mount Everest / by Kristen Rajczak.
p. cm. — (Thrill seekers)
Includes index.
ISBN 978-1-4824-6506-8 (pbk.)
ISBN 978-1-4824-3285-5 (6-pack)
ISBN 978-1-4824-0142-4 (library binding)
1. Everest, Mount (China and Nepal) — Juvenile literature. 2. Mountaineering — Everest, Mount (China and Nepal)
— History — Juvenile literature. 3. Everest, Mount (China and Nepal) — Discovery and exploration — Juvenile
literature. 4. Mountaineering — Everest, Mount (China and Nepal) — History. I. Rajczak, Kristen. II. Title.
GV199.44.E85 R35 2014
796.522—dc23

First Edition

Published in 2014 by
Gareth Stevens Publishing
111 East 14th Street, Suite 349
New York, NY 10003

Copyright © 2014 Gareth Stevens Publishing

Designer: Michael J. Flynn
Editor: Therese Shea

Photo credits: Cover, pp. 1, 19 STR/AFP/Getty Images; p. 5 (main) Pichugin Dmitry/Shutterstock.com; p. 5 (map)
Olinchuk/Shutterstock.com; p. 7 Prakash Mathema/AFP/Getty Images; p. 9 (Mount Everest) Pal Teravagimov/
Shutterstock.com; p. 9 (Hillary) Popperfoto/Getty Images; p. 9 (Tenzing) Baron/Hulton Archive/Getty Images;
p. 11 (climb in snow) Vixit/Shutterstock.com; p. 11 (rock climbing) Greg Epperson/Shutterstock.com;
p. 12 Galyna Andrushko/Shutterstock.com; p. 13 Morozov67/Shutterstock.com; p. 15 Christine Pemberton/
Getty Images; p. 17 Harry Kikstra/Flickr/Getty Images; p. 18 Meiquianbao/Shutterstock.com; pp. 21, 23
Jason Maehl/Flickr/Getty Images; p. 25 Hyoung Chang/Denver Post/Getty Images; p. 26 Lobo Press/
Peter Arnold/Getty Images; p. 29 Patrick Poendl/Shutterstock.com.

Printed in the United States of America

CPSIA compliance information: Batch #CW14GS: For further information contact Gareth Stevens, New York, New York at 1-800-542-2595.

CONTENTS

3 1886 00199 6326

Words in the glossary appear in **bold** type
the first time they are used in the text.

THE DEADLIEST DAY

On May 10, 1996, Neal Beidleman guided a group of climbers as they made their final ascent to the peak of Mount Everest. Beidleman had successfully reached the top, or summit, of the mountain before. But on this day, three different groups were making their way up the ice and snow to stand on top of the world as the wind was rising.

A blizzard struck. Some climbers, including several **amateurs**, couldn't make it to the camp thousands of feet below them. When it was over, eight were dead, and several more were **frostbitten** or injured in other ways.

One of Many

Mount Everest is found on the border of Nepal and Tibet. It's part of the Himalayas, a large mountain range in Asia. Though Everest is the tallest peak in the Himalayas, the mountain range has more than 110 mountains taller than

More than 3,000 people have reached Everest's summit.
Thousands more have tried and failed.

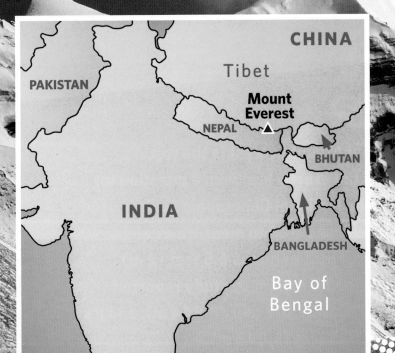

CHINA

Tibet

PAKISTAN

Mount
Everest

NEPAL

BHUTAN

INDIA

BANGLADESH

Bay of
Bengal

Beidleman was lucky to escape Everest's summit with his life. In 2011, he faced the ascent once more, hoping to make peace with his memories. After the climb, Beidleman said, "Being there again this year confirmed to me that [the 1996 tragedy] can happen again and happen very easily."

Why would Beidleman—or anyone else—tackle the climb to Everest's summit after the tragedy in 1996? For these thrill seekers, facing the danger makes the climb even more exciting and appealing. Since Mount Everest was first named the tallest point on Earth in the 1850s, people all over the world have challenged themselves to reach the top.

How High?

There's no question that Mount Everest is the world's tallest mountain. How tall *exactly* has been a question for many years. In 1999, the National Geographic Society used global positioning **satellites** (GPS) to measure a height of 29,035 feet (8,850 m) plus or minus 6.5 feet (2 m), depending on snow. In 2005, a Chinese study reported Everest's "rock height" was 29,017 feet (8,844 m), and its "snow height" was 29,028 feet (8,848 m).

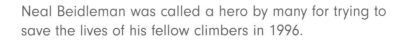
Neal Beidleman was called a hero by many for trying to save the lives of his fellow climbers in 1996.

REACHING THE TOP

Expeditions to Mount Everest began in the 1920s. Just getting to the mountain was hard, much less finding a way up it! But in 1953, Edmund Hillary and Tenzing Norgay scaled the nearly vertical ice formation that leads to the summit, becoming the first to do so.

In mid-May 1953, their group had established a camp high enough to try for the summit several times if they needed to. Two other climbers tried and failed to reach the summit on May 27. So, on May 29, Hillary and Tenzing set out early. As they climbed, they faced terrifying sheer drops, slick ice, and deadly rocks—but they made history.

Lost on Everest

Almost 30 years before Hillary and Tenzing's success, George Mallory attempted to climb the mountain for a third time. When asked why, he said, "Because it is there." He set out with another climber, Andrew Irvine, on the morning of June 8, 1924. Neither returned. Irvine's axe was discovered a few years later. Mallory's body wasn't found until 1999.

Hillary and Tenzing spent about 15 minutes at the top of Mount Everest. They shook hands and hugged when they finally reached it.

Edmund Hillary

Tenzing Norgay

NO TRAIN, NO GAIN

As exciting as reaching Everest's summit may sound, it takes an incredible amount of fitness just to reach the **base camp**, which is 17,600 feet (5,364 m) up! Therefore, it's important to train for the climb.

Climbers training for Everest—or any tall peak—focus on increasing endurance and strength. Running and hiking are a good place to start. Climbers often run up the stairs of a tall building to gain endurance, too. Hiking or doing shorter climbs with a heavy backpack helps increase strength. Some even pull a heavy sled through the snow to get ready!

Get Fit!

Most Everest climbs are attempted with a group through a company with experienced guides. Companies may reject interested climbers because of medical conditions or lack of fitness. Some companies require that climbers take a training course. They often provide an outline of how to get into Everest-climbing shape, too.

According to one company that leads Everest expeditions, climbers often say they misjudged the amount of fitness needed to reach the summit.

Climbing other mountains is the best way to train for Everest, and some climbers take years to work up to the highest peak in the world. Mount Washington in New Hampshire and Mount Rainier in Washington State are popular training grounds. Some Everest expedition companies suggest that climbers complete bigger climbs before attempting Everest, such as Mount McKinley, or Denali, in Alaska.

These experiences help climbers learn to withstand very high **altitudes**. Above 26,000 feet (7,925 m), there's a dangerous lack of oxygen. Increasingly higher climbs show climbers how their bodies react and how quickly they can **acclimate** to such a tall summit.

Mount McKinley

Mount McKinley, or Denali, is 20,320 feet (6,194 m) high.

Climbers must learn how to climb in ice and snow to prepare for what the highest parts of Everest are like.

Supplemental Oxygen

Until 1978, no one had reached Everest's summit without **supplemental** oxygen. It was thought to be impossible! Then, Reinhold Messner and Peter Habeler reached the summit with nothing but the air they breathed. Sound scary? It should. The air at the summit of Everest has only about a third as much oxygen as there is at sea level.

13

A lot of gear is needed to climb up Mount Everest! From a climbing **harness** and a **belay** device to an ice axe, much of it is specialized. Climbers should have experience with this gear before their climb. Here's a list of some of the other important supplies:

- two down sleeping bags
- large tent for base camp and lightweight tent to carry to higher camps
- headlamp with spare bulbs and batteries
- ski goggles
- compass or GPS unit

Each climber also needs socks, gloves, and jackets of varying thicknesses. Expedition companies often supply the climbing ropes, anchors, and rescue and medical gear, as well as other high-altitude supplies—like oxygen.

Alpine Siege

Many early climbers had military backgrounds. These "siege" climbers established camps at increasingly higher altitudes up a mountain for big groups to travel between. In the 1970s, many climbers returned to an earlier style of climbing known as "Alpine." Only three or four climbers ascended together as quickly as possible, carrying all their gear with them. Both ways are used to climb Everest today.

Climbers' packs may weigh about 30 pounds (14 kg) and commonly contain only the supplies and gear needed for the day.

ON TOP OF THE WORLD

April and May are the best months to climb Mount Everest. The amount of snow at the top is less then, and the wind and temperatures are more bearable. However, at the highest elevations, it still can be below freezing. The wind may blow 100 miles (160 km) per hour at the summit. Frostbite and **hypothermia** are risks every Everest climber faces in these conditions, even if they're dressed warmly.

Heat can be a problem, too! The Western Cwm (COOM), a deep valley some climbers cross, has little wind and such a high altitude that direct sunlight makes it very hot!

The Sherpas

Since the first Everest expeditions, the Sherpas (or Sharwa) who live around the mountain have served as guides. They're well adapted to the high altitudes and are often hired to carry supplies for climbing groups. Climbers may even hire their own personal Sherpa! Today, Everest expeditions and tourism are an important part of

Climbing Mount Everest is the ultimate packing challenge. Expedition companies recommend bringing many layers of clothing for possible temperature changes.

There are about 15 different routes from the base of Mount Everest to the summit. Most trips up the mountain take about 2 1/2 months. Much of this time is spent climbing to camps located on the side of the mountain, and then climbing increasingly higher in order to acclimate properly.

While hundreds of people try to reach the summit each year, many fail. Between the final camp and the summit is the Hillary Step, named for Edmund Hillary. Only one person can ascend or descend at a time. Those lucky daredevils who do make it to the top usually spend about 1 hour on the summit.

Fixed Ropes

The quest to Everest's summit has gotten somewhat easier over the years. The climbing ropes on the Hillary Step are fixed to the mountain ahead of time, so climbers just "clip in" to reach the summit. It's said to save time, but some serious climbers see it as "cheating" their way up such a famous peak.

These climbers attempt the Hillary Step. They're very close to reaching their goal!

ADDITIONAL COSTS

To some, paying the hefty price tag of climbing Mount Everest is just as risky as the climb. Joining a group that's ascending with an expedition company can cost more than $100,000! In addition, most companies don't offer refunds to those who don't reach the summit. So climbers aren't just in danger of injury—they're in danger of losing a lot of money. And that doesn't include the price of **insurance**, which is important to buy before heading to Everest.

The cost doesn't end there. Climbers have to pay to travel and buy much of their own gear. Training—such as climbing other big peaks—can be pricey, too.

What's for Dinner?

Expedition companies often provide food for their climbers. Meals include soup, rice, meat, and pasta—and even tea with milk and sugar! Water is often provided, too. Sometimes the Sherpas or staff cook. Other times, climbers use a small camp stove to cook meals. Climbers bring their own snack bars to eat during the climb.

While some expeditions cost "just" $35,000, that's still more than the price of many new cars!

OTHER DANGERS

Can climbers fall while climbing Mount Everest? Safety precautions are taken, but on Mount Everest, there are many places where you really need to watch your step. For those with a taste for danger, the South Route takes climbers up Khumbu Icefall. Falling ice, **avalanches**, and deep cracks make it one of the riskiest parts of the climb.

But perhaps the scariest part of ascending Everest is in each climber's mind. The fourth camp is located at the beginning of the "death zone," about 26,000 feet (7,925 m) up. Imagine trying to sleep at Camp IV, knowing your body may not be able to handle the altitude.

Altitude Sickness

The low oxygen levels high on Mount Everest can cause dizziness and trouble sleeping—or worse. Altitude sickness may lead to swelling of the brain, blackouts, fluid in the lungs, and more. Moving back down the mountain may help these conditions, but they're deadly if a climber isn't

Climbers may face Khumbu Icefall several times as they climb up and down the mountain, acclimating to the altitude.

FAMOUS CLIMBS

On May 22, 2010, Jordan Romero climbed to the summit of Mount Everest. He was already an experienced climber, having scaled some of the highest mountains in the world. But his climb up Everest was historic—Romero, an American, was only 13 years old!

The oldest person to ever climb Mount Everest was 80! A Japanese man named Yuichiro Miura ascended the highest peak on May 23, 2013. Watanabe Tamae, a Japanese woman, became the oldest woman to climb Everest at age 63 in 2002. Then, she broke her own record in 2012, scaling Everest at age 73.

A Lonely Climb

Reinhold Messner was one of the first people to climb Mount Everest without supplemental oxygen in 1978. Two years later, he reached the summit completely solo. Back at his tent, he was unable to eat or drink. After, he said, "I have never in my whole life been so tired as on the summit

Jordan Romero is the youngest person to ever reach
Everest's summit.

Anyone willing to risk their life on the side of Mount Everest is looking for the thrill of danger. But what about skiing down the side of such a huge mountain? That takes guts! In 2000, Davo Karničar completed the first entirely skied descent from the summit. Then, in 2001, Marco Siffredi descended by snowboard!

Many people find it challenging getting down Everest in boots. Just imagine wearing skis!

Other stunts have pushed climbers' mental and physical endurance to the max. In 1990, Tim Macartney-Snape walked from sea level at the Bay of Bengal to Everest's summit without extra oxygen. In 1996, Goran Kropp rode his bike from his home in Sweden to Everest, climbed the mountain, and then rode home!

Timeline of Mount Everest Firsts

1953 – Edmund Hillary and Tenzing Norgay are the first to Everest's summit.

1963 – The first Americans reach Everest's summit.

1975 – Tabei Junko from Japan is the first woman to reach the summit.

1978 – The first climbers reach Everest's summit without supplemental oxygen.

1980 – Reinhold Messner completes the first solo climb to Everest's summit.

2001 – Erik Weihenmayer is the first blind person to reach

FIND MORE THRILLS!

While climbers can't choose a climb *higher* than Everest, there are plenty of mountains around the world that offer tough, dangerous climbs!

K2, between China and Pakistan, is the second-tallest peak in the world, rising 28,251 feet (8,611 m). But some climbers say it's more daring to attempt K2 than Everest. Fewer people have climbed K2 than Everest, perhaps because its steepness and frequent storms make conditions even more challenging. But what's more telling is the death rate—the proportion of climbers who have died on K2 to those who have attempted the climb is much higher than that of Everest.

Seven Summits

Some daredevil climbers reach for a glory that surpasses conquering Everest—the Seven Summits. In addition to Mount Everest, this includes climbing Mount Elbrus in Russia, Aconcagua in Argentina, Mount McKinley in Alaska, Mount Kilimanjaro in Tanzania, Vinson Massif in Antarctica, and Carstensz Pyramid in Indonesia. Sometimes

Climbers say that a great climber can scale Everest—but one who reaches K2's summit is a "true climber to other climbers."

GLOSSARY

acclimate: to adapt to a new temperature, altitude, climate, environment, or situation

altitude: height above sea level

amateur: someone who has less experience doing something

avalanche: a large mass of snow sliding down a mountain or over a cliff

base camp: the first camp climbers reach when climbing a mountain

belay: having to do with securing a person to a rope

frostbitten: having damage to body parts caused by exposure to freezing conditions

harness: a set of straps fitted to a person to keep them in place

hypothermia: dangerously low body temperature caused by cold conditions

insurance: an agreement in which a person pays a company for a guarantee of money in case of harm, illness, or death

satellite: an object that circles Earth in order to collect and send information or aid in communication

siege: a long effort to overcome something

supplemental: additional

FOR MORE INFORMATION

BOOKS

Belanger, Jeff. *What It's Like to Climb Mount Everest, Blast Off Into Space, Survive a Tornado, and Other Extraordinary Stories.* New York, NY: Sterling Publishing, 2011.

Dickmann, Nancy. *Mount Everest.* Chicago, IL: Raintree, 2012.

Young, Jeff C. *Belaying the Line: Mountain, Rock, and Ice Climbing.* Edina, MN: ABDO Publishing, 2011.

WEBSITES

10 Tips for Safe Climbing
climbing.about.com/od/staysafeclimbing/tp/10ClimbingSafetyTips.htm
Do you want to learn to climb? These tips can help you be safe when you do!

Climbing Mount Everest
www.sciencekids.co.nz/videos/earth/mounteverest.html
Check out this video of climbers reaching the top of the highest peak in the world.

Everest Photos
adventure.nationalgeographic.com/adventure/everest/photo-galleries/
See tons of cool photographs taken by climbers on Mount Everest.

INDEX